Opening Activ

Before launching into a new unit, it is always a good idea to su
already know about the area to be studied. Ask your students
about their knowledge and experience with electricity:

We're going to do some safe activities with electricity.
Let's see what we can learn and we'll have some fun doing it...

Materials You'll Need

It doesn't take a scientific background or fancy scientific equipment to
teach and learn about basic principles of electricity.

For Current Electricity:

• 1 battery for each two students
Use the cheapest batteries.
Do not use alkaline batteries.
They heat the wires too much.

• 1 light bulb for each two students
Recommended or equivalent:
      Radio Shack   # 272-1120
      Radio Shack   # 272-1121

• Aluminum foil cut into 8" (20 mm) strips
about 1" (3 cm) wide. (This is your "wire")

• Masking tape

• Various materials for testing as conductors
or insulators (see page 6).

For Static Electricity:

• Balloons

• Nylon or wool cloth (cheap socks are good)

• Paper cut into confetti-sized pieces

• Salt or sugar

• String

• Plastic spoons

Bulbs, Batteries, and Wires

What is a light bulb?

Use the poster to show how a light bulb is constructed. Explain each part. Reproduce page 3 for your students to fill in as you discuss the parts of a light bulb. Have students look at a real bulb and compare it to the picture.

1. base — fits into socket of electricity source
2. electrodes — where electricity goes in or out
3. glass — protects wires and filament
4. wires — carry electricity to and from the filament
5. filament — lights up when electricity goes through it
6. spacer — keeps wires from touching each other

Show the two spots where electricity can go either in or out when it flows through the bulb.

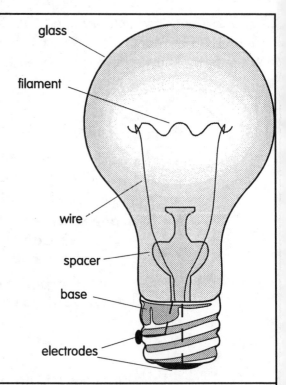

glass
filament
wire
spacer
base
electrodes

What is a battery?

Also use the poster to explain that a battery is a storage place for electricity. Explain to your students that the batteries you will be using are 1½ volts. This is not strong enough to hurt them. Point to the various battery parts and have your students fill in the names of the parts in this order:

1. battery case
2. electrode on each end
3. put a + on the end with the "bump"
4. put a - on the "flat" end
5. put "electricity goes in here" by the + end
6. put "electricity comes out here" by the - end

Have your students compare their drawing to a real battery.

electrode
electricity goes in here
battery case
electrode
electricity comes out here

What is a wire?

Anything made out of metal can act as a wire. You will be using strips of aluminum foil to create wire for the activities in this book. Provide your students with 6" x 1" (15 X 2.5 cm) strips of foil, and have them roll the foil into pieces of 6" (15cm) wire. Provide enough foil strips for each student to make 2 wires.

 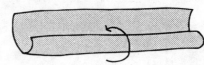 

Bulbs, Batteries, and Wires

What is a light bulb?

Write labels:

Describe what it does:

[ ] _____

[ ] _____

[ ] _____

[ ] _____

[ ] _____

[ ] _____

What is a battery?

Write labels

Describe what happens:

[ ] _____

[ ] _____

[ ] _____

What is a wire?

A wire is anything that _____.

Making a Circuit

What is a Circuit?

In order to flow, electricity has to have someplace to go. Draw the picture on the lower left-hand side of this page on the chalkboard for your students to see. Show them how the electricity is flowing in a circle. We call a circle of electricity a "circuit". Demonstrate the circuit you have drawn and show your students how it makes the bulb light up.

Making Circuits

Materials:
- battery
- bulb
- wire (You will be using strips of aluminum foil. See page 2 for directions.)

Have your students arrange a battery, wire, and bulb as you do in your demonstration to form circuit #1 below. This can be done individually or in groups, depending on the amount of materials with which you have to work. If your students arrange their set of items as your picture shows, the bulb will light. After all of the students have succeeded, demonstrate how to make the circuits shown on the reproducible student sheet on page 5. Have the students make all four of the circuits at the top of the page. Then, have them predict before trying the bottom two.

> Caution: Tell your students not to make a circuit without a bulb in it. When there is nothing in a circuit to slow down the current, it gets going too fast, and heats up the wire. This is called a "short circuit." Tell the students to disconnect any wire if it feels hot. Water can also cause current to flow too fast. Keep water away from your batteries and circuits.

Demonstrating the Circuit-testing Procedure

After your students understand the concept of a circuit, and how the bulb lighting up tells them they have created a complete circuit, they can play the prediction game shown on the poster. You will need to reproduce the cards on page 16 to use with the game. The instructions for the game are given on the inside back cover. Demonstrate how to play the game using the first two cards.

The arrangement on the first card is a complete circuit, and the bulb will light.

The arrangement on the second card is not a complete circuit, and the bulb will not light.

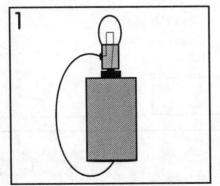

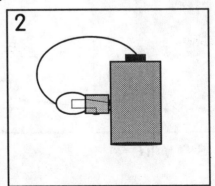

See the inside back cover for the poster card game instructions and the list of answers.

Making a Circuit

Create circuits to match these pictures.
All four of these should light the bulb.

Check here
if you got it
to light up.

Check here
if you got it
to light up.

Check here
if you got it
to light up.

Check here
if you got it
to light up.

Are These Circuits?

Mark your predictions. Then try each arrangement. The bulb will tell you if your predictions were right.

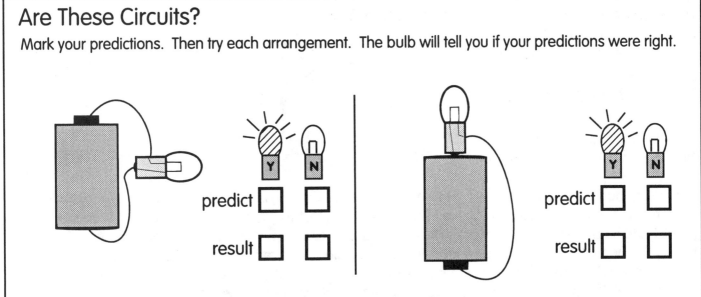

predict ☐ ☐

result ☐ ☐

predict ☐ ☐

result ☐ ☐

Conductors and Insulators

What is a conductor?

When electricity moves easily through something, we call it a conductor. Materials that conduct electricity are used to make wire for electrical circuits.

What is an insulator?

When eletricity does not move easily through something, we call it an insulator. Materials that do not conduct electricity are helpful too. They can be used to surround or cover electrical wiring to protect us from getting a shock.

Build an Open Circuit

Check to see if any of your students already know about conductors and insulators. Explain what each term means, then do the following demonstrations.

Put together a circuit as shown here with a gap in the circuit. Before beginning each of the three demonstrations, ask your students, "Will this object be a conductor or an insulator?" Talk about what they might consider in makingtheir predictions. Then, demonstrate these three tests:

Check the Circuit

Put a piece of your aluminum wire in the gap to make sure the bulb lights up when the circuit is complete.

Test a Conductor

Try a paper clip in the gap.
Does the bulb light up?
Yes. The paper clip is a conductor.

Test an Insulator

Put a rubber band in the gap.
Does the bulb light up?
No. The rubber band is an insulator.

wrap wire around bulb base here

hold bulb by the wire here

put item to be tested in here

tape wire to battery here

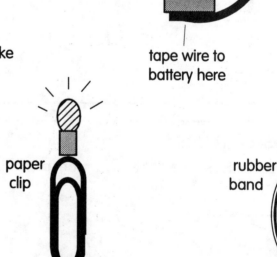

paper clip

rubber band

Reproduce page 7 for your students. Have them work individually, in pairs or in small groups to duplicate the three tests you demonstrated above. Then have them test 10 other common items. Remind them to predict and record whether each item will be a conductor or insulator before performing the test. Then have them place the items in two piles, conductors and insulators, and record the results on their observation page. After the activity, students can describe for the class what they tested and what the results were. If you have an electricity learning center, you could provide other items to be tested.

Are these conductors or insulators?

Name _____

Date _____

Observe carefully as your teacher demonstrates how to test items to find out if they are conductors or not. Before each demonstration, draw the item in the box and name it below. Then record your prediction to the right. After each demonstration, record the result.

predict ☐ ☐

result ☐ ☐

item:_____

predict ☐ ☐

result ☐ ☐

item:_____

Now test some items of your own choice, such as a penny, a piece of cloth, an eraser, a pencil, a pen, a glue stick, a jar, a lid, a comb, a rock, a piece of paper, string, or yarn. Remember to draw a picture of each item to be tested and write its name below. Then, record your prediction before doing the test. Finally, record the result.

predict ☐ ☐

result ☐ ☐

item:_____

predict ☐ ☐

result ☐ ☐

item:_____

predict ☐ ☐

result ☐ ☐

item:_____

predict ☐ ☐

result ☐ ☐

item:_____

predict ☐ ☐

result ☐ ☐

item:_____

predict ☐ ☐

result ☐ ☐

item:_____

© 1994 Evan-Moor Corp.

Electricity

What Is Electricity, Anyway?

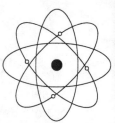

Jumping Electrons!

Discuss the concept of atoms with your students. They will have varying levels of prior knowledge. Be prepared to give a brief explanation of what atoms are. Everything that exists is made of atoms. The atoms are very small. In fact, they are so small, there are trillions of them on a pinhead. Around each atom are electrons. The electrons go around atoms like planets go around the sun.

Because electrons are away from the center of the atom, they can take off and jump to other atoms. When electricity flows through a wire, free electrons are jumping from one atom to the next, and to the next. Electrons flow this way along a wire.

Electrons can't just flow in a line. If they did, the last atom would end up with all of the electrons, and the current would stop. In order to flow, electrons have to have someplace to go. With a circuit, the electrons can flow around in a circle and back to the battery.

Class Activity:

Sit some or all of your students in a circle. Give each student a ball or a block of the same size. The students represent atoms. The balls or blocks represent electrons. Have one student (an atom) begin the demonstration by passing an "electron" to the next "atom." Tell the atoms that they can't hold on to two electrons. If they receive one, they have to pass the other electron on. A chain reaction will start, and the electrons will flow around the circle. It is a complete circuit.

Assign one student the role of a battery. Have the "battery" pass in three extra electrons (blocks) one at at time. Three electrons will have to come out at the other end, but they won't be the same three that were passed in.

Assign another student the role of a buzzer. He/She will buzz as long as he or she keeps receiving and passing on electrons (balls or blocks).

Player 1

1 Correct Prediction	2 Correct Predictions	3 Correct Predictions	4 Correct Predictions

If your prediction is correct, put the card on your playing board.

I predict the bulb will light up.

YES

Put the card here

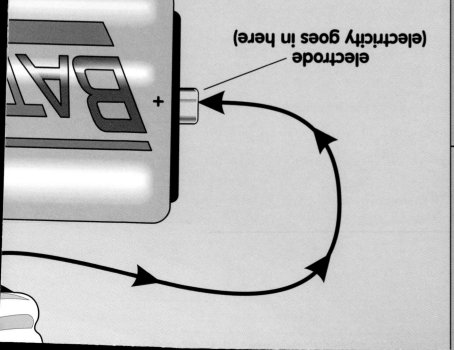

electrode (electricity goes in here)

+

BA

Is
Complet

**Take tu
predi
testir**

8 Correct
Predictions

7 Correct
Predictions

6 Correct
Predictions

5 Correct
Predictions

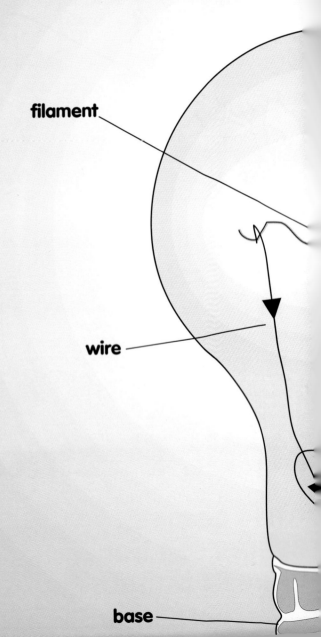

filament

wire

base

How Does a Switch Work?

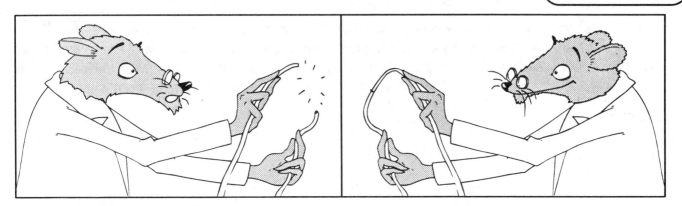

Completing or Breaking a Circuit

If there is a gap in part of a circuit, the electrons won't flow. To get them going, you have to close the gap, which is called "completing" a circuit. When you want to turn the flow of electricity off, you just have to make a gap in the wire, so the electrons can't keep flowing. This is called "breaking" a circuit.

Class Activity:

Use your circle of students playing atoms again (see page 8). As they are passing the electrons around, move some of the students apart so that they can't reach each other. The shape of your group will have changed from a circle to a horseshoe shape. Explain that the atoms can't throw the electrons, they can only pass them. Since there is a gap in the circuit that prevents passing the electrons, the flow of electrons stops.

Switches Make It Easy

Show your students how they can make a switch. They will need to make a circuit with a battery, bulb, and wire, as before, but this time they leave an opening in the wire. The gap in the wire serves as an "off" switch and their light bulb will not light up. When they make the two loose ends touch, it forms an "on" switch and their bulb will light. When they pull the two ends apart, the bulb goes out again.

When you flip a wall switch, the wires are separated inside the wall. That stops the flow of electricity, and the room lights go off.

A Special Kind of Switch

If wires that aren't supposed to touch inside an appliance do touch each other accidentally, the electrons can take a "shortcut." Without the full circuit to slow them down, they get going too fast, heat up the wire, and cause a special kind of switch to go off to prevent a fire. There are two kinds of special switches that do this:

   • A "fuse" melts and makes a gap in the circuit. To get the electricity back on, you have to put in a new fuse.

   • A "circuit breaker" expands when heated and turns off a switch. To get the electricity back on, you don't have to put in a new breaker. You can just reset it.

In either case, there's no use replacing or resetting unless you fix the short circuit first. Otherwise, the power will just be cut off again.

What Is Static Electricity?

Everything is made of atoms. Atoms have about the same number of positive (+) and negative (-) particles. The positive particles (protons) are in the middle where they can't get out and run around. The negative particles (electrons) are on the outside where they can come and go. When free electrons flow through a conductor, we call that "current" electricity. When extra electrons collect and stay in an object for a period of time, we call that "static" electricity.

There are two kinds of static charges.

• When an object has a lot of extra electrons, the object is said to have a **negative** (-) charge.

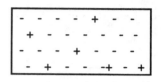

• When an object has lost electrons, the object is left with extra protons, so it is said to have a **positive** (+) charge.

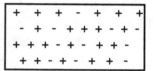

Clouds often have static charges. Some are negative and some are positive. The air around the clouds acts as an insulator, so the electric charge gets trapped in the cloud. When clouds with different charges get close enough to each other, the cloud with too many electrons can "zap" some over to a nearby cloud with too few electrons or to the ground as a bolt of lightning.

This is a sticky situation.

Unlike charges attract. Like charges repel.

Even if your students don't do the laundry, they've seen plenty of "static cling" on television commercials. Students can see miniature lightning by darkening the laundry area and pulling clinging socks apart slowly when they first come out of the dryer. When objects are rubbed together in dry air, some objects tend to give electrons to other objects. The object that gained electrons gets a negative charge. The object that lost electrons is left with a positive charge. The objects are attracted to each other in an attempt to equalize their charges. That's what is happening when the sparks fly.

Object with opposite charges move toward each other. They are trying to trade electrons. Objects with the same charge push each other away. They're both trying to give electrons away, or they're both trying to get electrons.

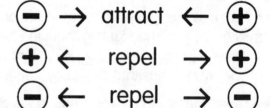

Have your students complete the activities on page 11. After they have recorded the results, conduct a discussion to develop the concepts described above. Have students write their conclusions at the bottom of their activity sheets to confirm what they have learned about static electricity.

Note: These experiments don't work well on humid days. The drier the weather, the better they will work.
Try out the activities yourself on the day before, or the morning of the day you plan to use them.

                                                                               Electricity

Experimenting with Static Electricity

Name _____

Date _____

Most objects have about the same number of positive and negative particles, so they have a neutral charge. When objects get out of balance by losing or gaining electrons, they act funny. Try these little experiments to see what we mean.

Here's what you do:

Draw or write what happens:

Rub a balloon several times against nylon or wool. Then hold the rubbed side of the balloon close to some salt sprinkled on the table. Watch closely and listen to the sounds that are produced.

Rub a plastic comb through your hair several times. Then hold the comb near, but not touching your hair. Does dry hair act differently than wet hair? Hold the comb next to small bits of torn paper.

Try it with a rubbed balloon too.

Suspend a plastic spoon with a piece of thread. Rub one end of the suspended spoon with silk or wool cloth. Now rub one end of another spoon with the same cloth. Hold the rubbed end up to one end of the suspended spoon without touching it. Be careful not to touch the rubbed ends of the spoons with your hands. What happens? Hold the same end of the hand-held spoon near the other end of the suspended spoon. What happens now?

After you have recorded your results and have had a discussion about what happened and why, complete these sentences about static electricity.

Unlike charges _____

Like charges _____

Safety with Current Electricity

Electric Shocks

Explain to your students that water carries electricity almost as well as metal. With water, the electricity has even more directions the electrons can go. As a result, water can hold a lot of electricity. Water and electricity are a dangerous combination.

Here's another important fact to remembr. Your body is mostly water! That means that you are a conductor of electricity too! If you touch water that has electricity flowing into it, you can become part of the circuit and be badly hurt. If you touch something that has electric current coming out of it, the electrons can jump to you and you will get a shock. If you are standing in, or if you have your hand in water at the time, the situation is even worse. The electrons can go completely through your body and come out the other side to flow into the water. Instead of just a momentary pulse of electricity, the current can keep flowing through your body. Rather than just a shock, you could be killed. Remind your students that the batteries you will be using in the classroom are not stong enough to hurt you, but an electrical outlet can.

Class Activity:

Use Poster #2 to see if your students can recognize the electrical hazards shown and explain why they are dangerous. Have your students work in pairs to discuss what they see. Then come together for a class discussion about the hazards and how they can be avoided.

A. If the kite string touches the power line, electricity could flow down the string.

B. It is never safe to climb a power pole. When line-workers go up, they turn off the current first.

C. If a radio or TV falls into a pool, hot tub, or bathtub, anyone in the water could be electrocuted.

D. Never poke something into an electrical outlet. People who fix outlets turn off the power first.

E. A hair drier shouldn't be used when it could fall into a sink full of water. Empty the sink first.

F. If the tree pruner touches that wire, a shock could knock him right off the roof onto his head.

Safety With Current Electricity
These people are in danger. Explain why.

Insulators

Insulators are materials that don't conduct electricity. Insulators can help protect you from shocks. Any time there is a chance that you might become part of a circuit, you can help avoid the hazard by wearing or holding something that will break the current. That's why people who work around electricity wear rubber gloves and rubber-soled shoes, why they use tools with wood or plastic handles, and why they use wooden, rather than metal ladders.

Emphasize that no one should play around electrical wires even if they do have on rubber shoes or gloves. Insulators can help reduce electrical dangers, but there is no guarantee that they will work. There could be a hole in a glove or moisture on a shoe that would let the current through.

 Electricity

Safety with Static Electricity

Discuss these aspects of static electricity with your students. The rubbing together of materials can cause one material to gain electrons while the other loses them. If an object gets filled with a lot of extra electrons, it can neutralize its charge by releasing the electrons as a blast of energy such as lightning or an electric shock that can hurt you.

Here are two examples of how static electricity could jump from one object to another using *you* as the connection:

Lightning can use you as the connection between a cloud and the ground.	*A static charge can go through a truck driver when he steps onto the ground after driving through dry air.*

There are ways to help keep static charges from building up to a dangerous level:
- A lightning rod on a tall building gives electrons a path to flow to the ground.
- Big trucks drag a metal cord from the back bumper to let electrons flow between the truck and the ground.

Class Activity:

Use Poster #2 to see if your students can recognize the best and worst choices for avoiding being struck by lightning. Accept a few responses from your students without prior information. Then explain that lightning is most likely to strike tall things, water or wet things, and things that conduct electricity well. See what difference this information makes in their responses.

1. The house is tall, so it might be struck by lightning. Being next to it isn't nearly as safe as being in it.
2. Being in the house is a good idea, provided you stay away from the chimney, walls, and windows.
3. If that flagpole is metal, it is a great target for lightning. If it is wood, it still isn't the place to stand.
4. Trees are often struck by lightning because they are tall. Better not stand next to a target.
5. Standing in water makes you a better conductor than you already are. Get out of there fast!
6. Getting under those rocks seems like a good idea, but they make a tall target for lightning. Not a good place.
7. Holding up an umbrella or a golf club gives the lightning a tall, metallic target to strike. An umbrella with a wooden or plastic handle is safer, but would still make a taller target out of you.
8. That fellow looks like he's in danger lying out in the open, but he is safer that way than he would be if he were standing up.

Safety With Static Electricity

A lightning storm is coming!
Who is the safest person here?
Why are the others in danger?

In summary, the best place to be when lightning is very close is inside, but staying away from walls and windows. If you are out in the open, stay away from water or tall things, and make yourself short too. You don't want your students to be overly afraid during stormy weather, but to know what to do when lightning is striking right around them.

Where Does Our Electricity Come From?

When a magnet moves while it is next to a wire, it makes electrons flow along the wire. That means that we can make electricity if we can use some kind of force to keep the magnet moving next to the wire that leads to our houses and factories.

With "hydroelectric" power, river water is collected by a dam. The water goes down through a pipe and spins the turbine as it goes by.

Atomic power can be used to heat the water and the resulting steam is used to turn the turbine.

The usual way to do this is to attach the magnet to a propeller (called a turbine) and surround the magnet with coils of wire.

A variety of forces are used to spin the turbine:

Sometimes, river or sea water is heated. The steam that is produced goes through a pipe and turns the turbine.

The generator can be like a windmill with a turbine similar to an airplane propeller on top of a pole. Wind turns the propeller to make the electricity.

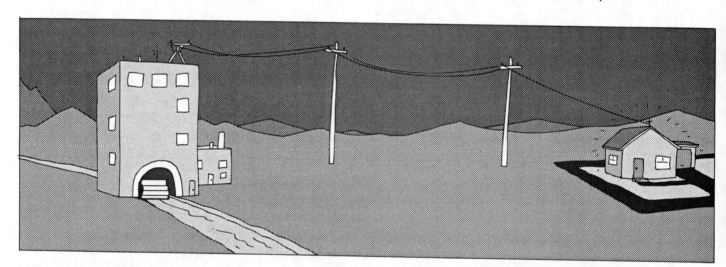

Machines that use a pushing force to make electricity by moving a magnet near coils of wire are called electric **generators**. Now here's an interesting question. Could this process be reversed? Could you use electricity in a wire to make the magnet spin and produce a force to push something? Yes! These kinds of devices are called electric **motors**.

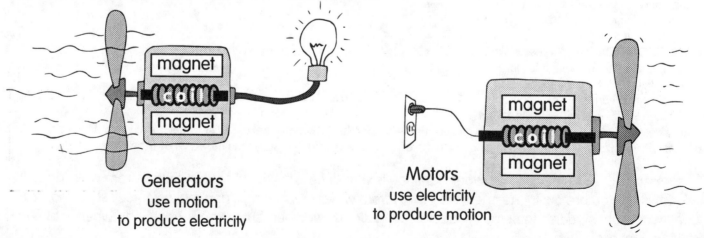

Generators
use motion
to produce electricity

Motors
use electricity
to produce motion

What Have I Learned?

Name _____

Date _____

Everything is made of _____. Flying around them are

_____. These _____ particles

can go from one place to another. When the electrons move to another object

and stay there, we call that stored energy _____ electricity, because it

isn't going anywhere. When electrons *flow* along a _____, we

call that _____ electricity. When electricity flows around in a

circle, we call that circle a _____. The thing we use to turn

the current on and off is called a _____. Material that won't

carry electricity is called an _____. Be careful around

electricity. It does important work for us, but it can be _____.

A device that makes electricity is called a _____.

A device that uses electricity to produce a force to move things is called a

_____.

current	electrons	insulator
generator	switch	atoms
static	motor	negative
dangerous	conductor	circuit

Which of these Are Complete Circuits?

Use these cards together with Poster #1 to do the activity described on the inside back cover.

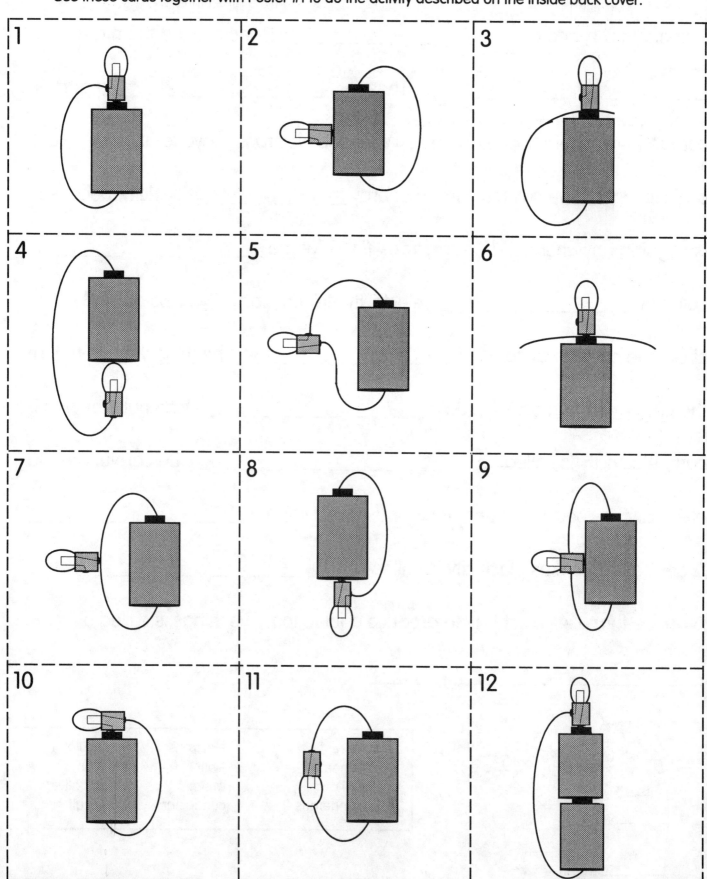

Electricity